My Home Country

POLAND

IS MY HOME

For a free color catalog describing Gareth Stevens' list of high-quality books, call 1-800-341-3569 (USA) or 1-800-461-9120 (Canada).

For their help in the preparation of *My Home Country: Poland Is My Home*, the author would like to thank Heddy Moskaluk of Polonia Travel Agency, who suggested the Sczaniecki family and helped with lodging arrangements; the Sczanieckis themselves for opening their home and family to me; Waldek Dynerman for arranging for my interpreter, Agnieszka Zieborak, and her assistant, Sławik Kojło, who interpreted, guided and drove me over much of Poland; and Janusz Tylman for his hospitality while I was in Warsaw. I also would like to thank my husband, Daniel, and son, Noah, for their love and support during my travels and writing and photographic endeavors.

Flag illustration on page 42, © Flag Research Center. Photograph of Pope John Paul II on page 34 courtesy of the Embassy of the Republic of Poland.

Library of Congress Cataloging-in-Publication Data

Holland, Gini.
    Poland is my home / adapted from Gini Holland's Children of the world—Poland by Gini Holland ; photographs by Gini Holland.
      p. cm. — (My home country)
    Includes bibliographical references and index.
    Summary: A look at the life of an eleven-year-old Polish girl and her parents living in Poznan. Includes a section with information on Poland.
    ISBN 0-8368-0904-1
    1. Poland—Juvenile literature. 2. Children—Poland—Juvenile literature. [1. Family life—Poland. 2. Poland.] I. Holland, Gini. Poland. II. Title. III. Series.
DK4147.H66 1993
943.8—dc20

92-30689

Edited, designed, and produced by

Gareth Stevens Publishing
1555 North RiverCenter Drive, Suite 201
Milwaukee, Wisconsin 53212, USA

Series editors: Barbara J. Behm and Beth Karpfinger
Cover design: Kristi Ludwig
Layout: Kate Kriege
Map design: Sheri Gibbs

Printed in the United States of America

1 2 3 4 5 6 7 8 9 97 96 95 94 93

My Home Country

POLAND
IS MY HOME

Adapted from
Children of the World: Poland
by Gini Holland
Photographs by Gini Holland

Gareth Stevens Publishing
MILWAUKEE

Eleven-year-old Matylda Sczaniecka lives with her parents and her dog on the top floor of an apartment building in Poznan, Poland. She learned to speak English in the United States and is studying the Russian and Polish languages in school. Matylda enjoys playing with her cousins and visiting other relatives. On Saturdays, Matylda likes to go to Poznan's town square to shop, eat ice cream, and take a horse-and-cart ride.

To enhance this book's value in libraries and classrooms, clear and simple reference sections include up-to-date information about Poland's history, land and climate, people and language, education, and religion. *Poland Is My Home* also features a large and colorful map, bibliography, glossary, simple index, research topics, and activity projects designed especially for young readers.

The living conditions and experiences of children in Poland vary according to economic, environmental, and ethnic circumstances. The reference section helps bring to life for young readers the diversity and richness of the culture and heritage of Poland. Of particular interest are discussions of Poland's rise from communist rule.

My Home Country includes the following titles:

Canada	*Nicaragua*
Costa Rica	*Peru*
Cuba	*Poland*
El Salvador	*South Africa*
Guatemala	*Vietnam*
Ireland	*Zambia*

CONTENTS

LIVING IN POLAND:
Matylda, Student of Languages

Eleven-year-old Matylda Sczaniecka and her parents live on the top floor of an apartment building in Poznan, Poland. Matylda's mother, Alicja, is a child psychologist. Her father, Bolek, is a physicist. The family has a dog named Babsy.

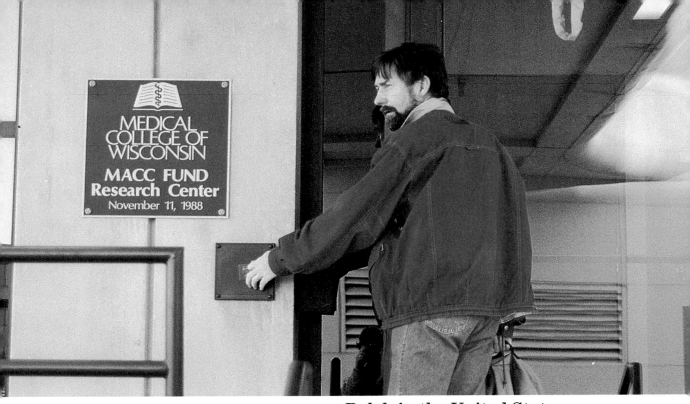

Bolek in the United States.

At times, Bolek's work takes him to other countries. Last year, Matylda and her mother joined him in the United States. There, Matylda learned English.

Matylda and her mother like to walk to church even in the rain.

As in most Polish cities, magnificent churches dominate Poznan's skyline.

Matylda tries to keep Babsy on a short leash as they pass their neighbors' gardens.

Matylda's Neighborhood and Home

Every morning, Babsy wakes Matylda to go for a walk. Matylda doesn't mind. She and Babsy go down the four flights of stairs in their apartment building. Then they walk past the playground, around the sandbox, and out onto a field. They enjoy playing in the open, grassy area.

Even in big cities, apartment buildings in Poland often have wooded paths nearby.

Apartment Life in Poland

More than half of the families in Poland live in apartments. There are more apartment buildings than houses because so many houses were bombed during World War II (1939-1945). When the former Soviet Union took over Poland after the war, apartment buildings were constructed to provide people with a place to live.

Apartments in Poland have balconies so that people can enjoy the outdoors.

After the war, each family in Poland had to request housing from the government. Matylda lives in a big apartment, but her family had to wait many years for it.

Many apartment neighbors garden side by side.

Alicja, Matylda's mother, works with children in a hospital. She tests them and tries to help them with their problems and feelings. After work, she shops for food and then takes the bus home. At home, she makes dinner and does the household chores. It is a long day, but fortunately, Matylda is willing to help out.

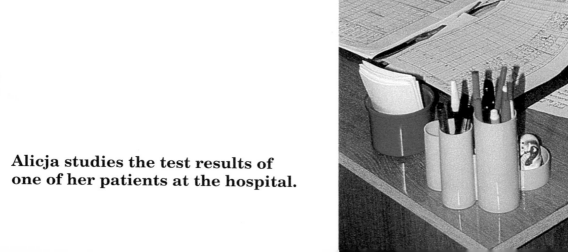

Alicja studies the test results of one of her patients at the hospital.

Bolek uses many machines and instruments in his research. This machine makes a graph that records the important findings of his experiments.

Matylda's father, Bolek, is a physicist at the Institute of Molecular Physics in Poznan. He uses machines to test scientific ideas. Bolek then develops reports that describe his findings.

Above: Matylda's grandfather and an aunt enjoy the times when Matylda comes to visit.

Matylda's grandmother always welcomes her with a warm smile. ▸

Matylda's Grandparents

On Sundays, Matylda and her mother walk to her grandparents' house for a visit. Matylda feels at home there. Her grandparents always ask Matylda about her schoolwork and the languages she is learning. They love to hear her stories.

Matylda can never leave without flowers to take home. Flowers are an important part of daily life in Poland. They are always for sale in the city squares. Most apartments have flower boxes, and all the homes have

The garden belonging to Matylda's grandparents has a large variety of flowers.

In the town squares of Poland, flower sellers do a big business. These flowers are for sale in the ancient capital city of Cracow.

flower gardens. People throughout Poland put flowers on war memorials and religious shrines every day.

School Days in Poland

Each weekday morning, Matylda says good-bye to her mother and Babsy. She then walks about six blocks to school.

After a happy summer, Matylda is not so sure she wants to go back to school. But her mother comforts Matylda and helps her make the best of it.

On the playground, Matylda and her friends have a chance to chat with their teacher from last year.

Matylda's school has about 350 students, with about 30 children in each class. The girls usually sit on one side of the classroom and the boys on the other. Each child must stand when speaking to the teacher.

Matylda sits near her friend Sylvia. They listen closely to the teacher and take notes.

21

Since it is the beginning of the school year, the classroom is bare except for a plaque on the wall of the Crowned Eagle, a symbol of Poland. Soon the walls will be covered with the students' artwork, posters, and maps.

When recess comes, Matylda and Sylvia walk arm-in-arm down the halls. They go outside and play jump rope with the other girls.

After recess, the rest of the day is spent on science, social studies, and the Russian and Polish languages.

Right, top: Like children everywhere, Matylda and her friends like to talk with one another before class begins.

Right, bottom: At recess, Matylda watches and gets ready for her turn at jumping rope.

World War II Still Affects Poles

The first day of September is usually the first day of school. But it is also a very sad day for Poland. It is the anniversary of the day when Nazi Germany's leader, Adolf Hitler, invaded Poland. This day marks the beginning of World War II.

Poland was once a center for Jewish culture in Europe. The Nazis tried to destroy this culture by putting Jews and other Poles into concentration camps.

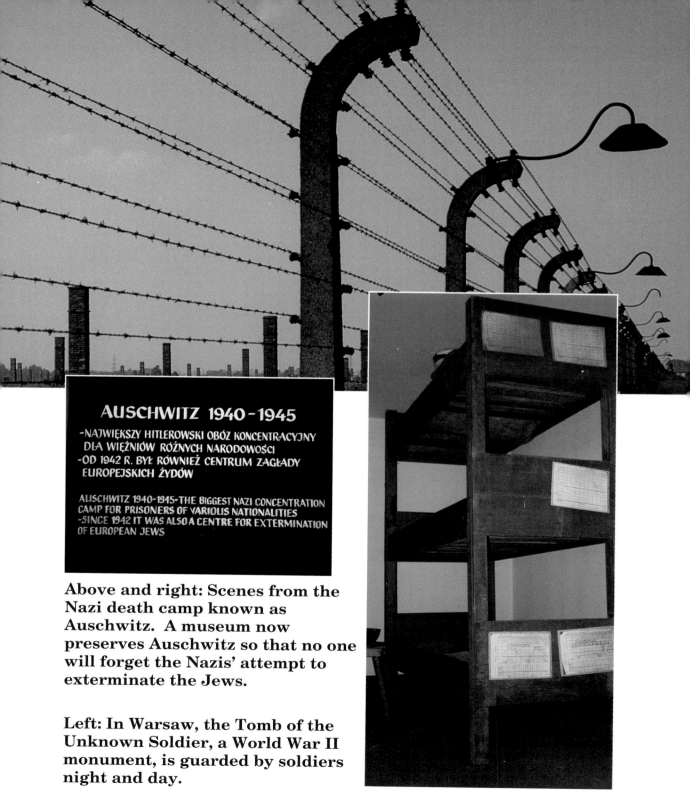

AUSCHWITZ 1940-1945

-NAJWIĘKSZY HITLEROWSKI OBÓZ KONCENTRACYJNY
DLA WIĘŹNIÓW RÓŻNYCH NARODOWOŚCI
-OD 1942 R. BYŁ RÓWNIEŻ CENTRUM ZAGŁADY
EUROPEJSKICH ŻYDÓW

AUSCHWITZ 1940-1945-THE BIGGEST NAZI CONCENTRATION
CAMP FOR PRISONERS OF VARIOUS NATIONALITIES
-SINCE 1942 IT WAS ALSO A CENTRE FOR EXTERMINATION
OF EUROPEAN JEWS

Above and right: Scenes from the Nazi death camp known as Auschwitz. A museum now preserves Auschwitz so that no one will forget the Nazis' attempt to exterminate the Jews.

Left: In Warsaw, the Tomb of the Unknown Soldier, a World War II monument, is guarded by soldiers night and day.

25

During this horrible time in the world's history, over three million Jews were killed in Poland alone.

Even now, more than fifty years later, Matylda's family remembers World War II well. Matylda's father was a young child at the start of the war. He will never forget how his family had to run away from the Nazis.

After the war, the Polish Communist Party, run by the

Artwork in Poland expresses dislike for the late communist leader Vladimir Lenin.

This poster shows the Polish word for *Solidarity*. Solidarity is the shipbuilders' union that helped lead the way to Polish democracy in the 1980s.

former Soviet Union, took over Poland. Years later, the Polish people worked to get the vote back for their own political parties. In 1989, Poland held its first free elections. The communists lost, setting Poland free.

In spite of the new political outlook for Poland, modern technology has not completely arrived. Many farmers in Poland still depend on horses to work the land and harvest crops.

Above: This horse-drawn cart circles Poznan's town square every Saturday. Below: Flowers are very important in the daily lives of the Polish people.

Poznan's Old Market Square

On Saturdays, Matylda often visits Poznan's town square. The historic homes that line the square were rebuilt after World War II. Art galleries, bookstores, clothing stores, and ice cream shops make a visit to the square fun.

Matylda also goes for a horse-and-cart ride. She enjoys listening to the clip-clop of the horse's shoes. She can imagine her grandmother doing this as a child.

Breads and fruits are plentiful in Poland, but sweet corn is a treat.

Art and Culture: Pałac Kultury

Matylda's handiwork: weaving (above) and a mask (below).

Just off the town square is a building called the Pałac Kultury. Matylda has studied art, dance, and weaving there. Her first project was to weave a picture of an apple. It turned out so well that her mother put it up in the front hall. When Matylda's father is away from home, she draws pictures for him. She sends him the pictures inside her letters.

◀ Even when she is not enrolled in art lessons at the Pałac Kultury, Matylda can still go to the movies there.

33

Sundays

On Sundays, Matylda goes to church with her parents. Once a month, the sermon is especially for young people. Matylda and her friends try to sit quietly while the priest speaks.

About 98 percent of Poland is Roman Catholic. This religion is a central part of life for most Polish people. Even the smallest town has at least one church. Religious shrines, decorated with ribbons and flowers, are placed at every crossroad throughout the entire country.

Poles are also very proud that Pope John Paul II, from Poland, was elected pope in 1978. Poles flock to see him during his visits to his homeland.

◀ **On a visit to Poland, Pope John Paul II prays at the Fallen Shipyard Workers monument in Gdansk. The monument honors strikers killed while protesting communist rule.**

Above: Matylda helps her
mother prepare for the
evening's company.

Right: Drying dishes is a
good time for Matylda to
chat with her mother.

Babsy always likes to lead Matylda and her cousins off their regular path.

Daily Chores

One of Matylda's chores is to set the table. After dinner, she helps with the dishes. It is also Matylda's job to take Babsy for a walk after school and again after dinner. Matylda's cousins, who live nearby, often join her on the walk with Babsy. Matylda thinks this chore is more fun than work.

Relaxing at Home

School is hard work. By the end of the day, Matylda is happy to

Matylda's cousin Krystina blows a bubble . . .

be at home playing with her cousins. They balance on her roller ball and play with toys.

gets into trouble!

Matylda also has a large collection of dolls.

Sometimes Matylda and her cousins play the board game of Monopoly. It is fun pretending to have all that money to spend.

Matylda and her cousins also enjoy watching television. Some of the shows they like to watch are broadcast all the way from the United States.

Even play can be serious when money is involved.

Fun at School

Watching television is fun, but playing outside during school recess is better. Often the children play a game of "Simon Says" with all the girls lined up on the steps. They have so much fun that it is sometimes hard to return to classes.

Matylda is happy to be back in school. She is enjoying this special time in her life, laughing and learning with her friends.

Matylda and her friends play "Simon Says" during recess.

MORE FACTS ABOUT: Poland

Official Name: Polska
                   (POHL-skuh)
                   Poland

Capital: Warsaw

History

Ancestors of today's Polish people were members of Slavonic tribes that settled in the heart of Europe. Over time, these tribes changed from primitive societies to highly developed, organized communities. By the mid-17th century, however, Poland was weak from wars with the countries surrounding it. The worst wars were with Islamic Turks, who wanted Poland to be part of their empire. Poland finally defeated them in 1683.

In the late 18th century, Poland's neighbors— Russia, Prussia, and Austria— joined forces and took Poland for their own. At that time, the country of Poland no longer existed.

At the end of World War I, Poland regained its independence. It was independent from 1918 until September 1, 1939, when Nazi Germany invaded Poland at the beginning of World War II. From 1945 until 1989, the former Soviet Union controlled Poland.

In 1980, the Polish labor movement, Solidarity, and its leader, Lech Walesa, began to protest communist control. Finally, in 1989, the communists allowed the Poles to elect officials from other political parties. Poland became an independent, democratic nation in 1990.

Land and Climate

Poland is about the size of New Mexico. Three-fifths of the country is farmland. Winters are cold with heavy snow. Summers are warm with moderate rainfall. The coast has milder weather than inland.

People and Language

Poland has about 37.5 million people. Ninety-eight percent of them are Polish-speaking Slavs.

Education

School is free and required for students from ages 7 through 15. About 98 percent of all Poles over the age of 15 can read and write.

Religion

About 94 percent of Poles are Roman Catholic. The remainder are Russian Orthodox, Protestant, or Jewish. In 1978, Pope John Paul II was elected the first pope from Poland.

Sports and Recreation

As with most countries in Europe, soccer is the top sport in Poland. Poles also enjoy basketball, volleyball, and tennis. Other popular forms of recreation include sailing, mountain climbing, skiing, and horseback riding.

Polish People in North America

Polish migration to the United States and Canada began after 1850. Chicago, Illinois, now has more Poles than does Warsaw, the capital of Poland. Ontario, Canada, also has large communities of Polish people.

The basic unit of money in Poland is the złoty.

44

Glossary of Useful Polish Terms

dziekuje bardzo (jen-KOO-ya BARD-zo): thank you very much

dzie´n dobry (jen DOB-ree): good morning

prosze bardzo (PRASH-uh BARD-zo): you are welcome

More Books about Poland

Poland. Greene (Childrens Press)
Take a Trip to Poland. Lye (Franklin Watts)

Things to Do

1. Pretend you are in Poland and dealing with Polish money. Set up your own store, and mark all the merchandise with prices in złoties. Make your own "play" złoty.

2. If you would like a Polish pen pal, write to Worldwide Pen Friends, P.O. Box 39097, Downey, CA, 90241.

Be sure to tell them what country you want your pen pal to be from. Also include your full name, age, and address.

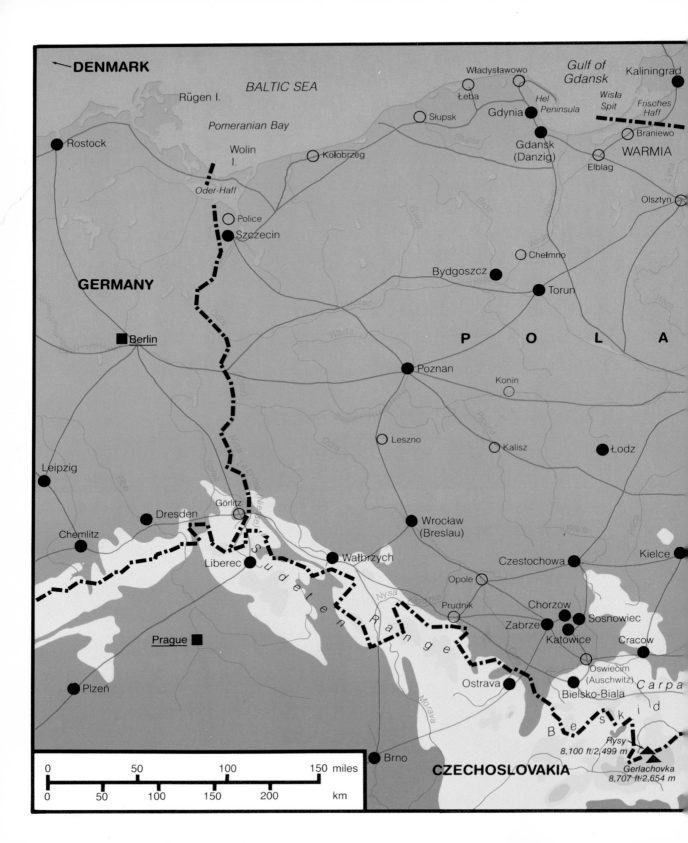

POLAND – Political and Physical

USSIA

Pregolya

LITHUANIA

Vilnius

Goldap

Mamo

Grodno

Solarowy

Kolno

BELARUS

Białystok

N

D

Bug

Warsaw

Brest

Pripyat

Wisła

Radom

Lublin

Wieprz

Chełm

San

Tarnow

Rzeszow

Wisła

Przemysl

L'vov

Mountains

Dniester

UKRAINE

Ondava

Crops, Industry, and Natural Resources

- ◖ Coal
- 🐟 Fishing
- 🌾 Grains
- 🐂 Livestock
- ⊠ Oil
- Potatoes
- Sugar Beets

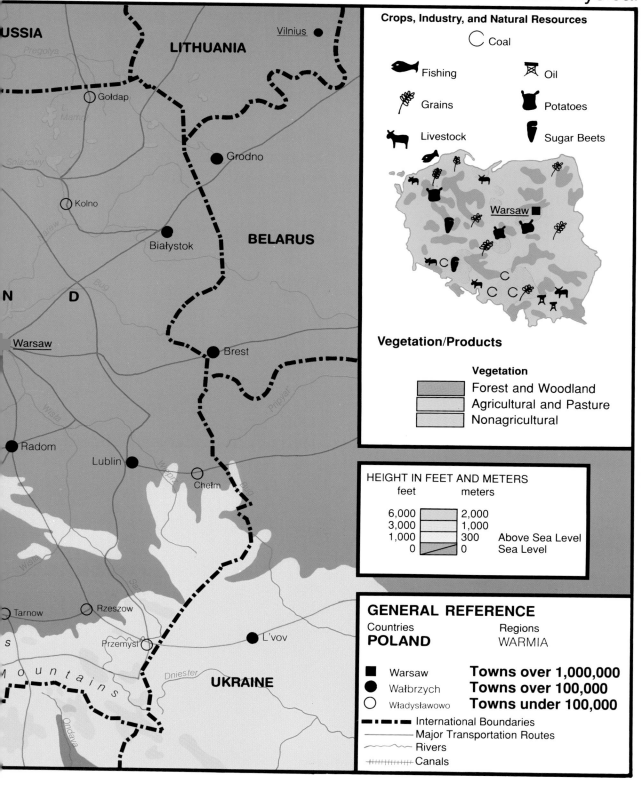

Warsaw

Vegetation/Products

Vegetation

▓	Forest and Woodland
░	Agricultural and Pasture
▒	Nonagricultural

HEIGHT IN FEET AND METERS

feet		meters	
6,000		2,000	
3,000		1,000	
1,000		300	Above Sea Level
0		0	Sea Level

GENERAL REFERENCE

Countries	Regions
POLAND	WARMIA

■ Warsaw	**Towns over 1,000,000**
● Wałbrzych	**Towns over 100,000**
○ Władysławowo	**Towns under 100,000**
▬ ▪ ▬ ▪ ▬	International Boundaries
——	Major Transportation Routes
∿∿	Rivers
┼┼┼┼┼	Canals

Index